THE WYNONA STONE POEMS

ABOUT THE LEXI RUDNITSKY EDITOR'S CHOICE AWARD

The Lexi Rudnitsky Editor's Choice Award is a collaboration between Persea Books and The Lexi Rudnitsky Poetry Project. It sponsors the annual publication of a poetry collection by an American who has published at least once previous full-length book of poems. The Editor's Choice Award is the second collaboration between Persea and the Lexi Rudnitsky Poetry Project, following the Lexi Rudnitsky First Book Prize in Poetry, awarded annually to an American woman who has yet to publish a book. Both awards are conducted via contest. Entry guidelines are available on Persea's website.

Lexi Rudnitsky (1972–2005) grew up outside of Boston, and studied at Brown University and Columbia University. Her own poems exhibit both a playful love of language and a fierce conscience. Her writing appeared in *The Antioch Review, Columbia: A Journal of Literature and Art, The Nation, The New Yorker, The Paris Review, Pequod,* and *The Western Humanities Review.* In 2004, she won the Milton Kessler Memorial Prize for Poetry from *Harpur Palate.*

Lexi died suddenly in 2005, just months after the birth of her first child and the acceptance for publication of her first book of poems, *A Doorless Knocking into Night* (Mid-List Press, 2006). The Lexi Rudnitsky book prizes were created to memorialize her by promoting the type of poet and poetry in which she so spiritedly believed.

PREVIOUS WINNERS OF THE LEXI RUDNITSKY EDITOR'S CHOICE AWARD:

2012   Michael White, *Vermeer in Hell*
2011   Mitchell L. H. Douglas, *blak al-febet*
2010   Amy Newman, *Dear Editor*

THE WYNONA STONE POEMS

CAKI WILKINSON

Winner of the 2013 Lexi Rudnitsky Editor's Choice Award

A Karen & Michael Braziller Book

PERSEA BOOKS / NEW YORK

Persea Books, Inc.
277 Broadway
New York, NY 10007

Library of Congress Cataloging-in-Publication Data
Wilkinson, Caki, 1980–
[Poems. Selections]
The Wynona Stone poems / Caki Wikinson.—First edition.
    pages ; cm
"A Karen & Michael Braziller Book."
"Winner of the 2013 Lexi Rudnitsky Editor's Choice Award."
ISBN 978-0-89255-446-1 (original trade pbk. : alk. paper)
I. Title.
PS3623.I553A6 2014
811'.6—dc23
              2014022625

First edition
Printed in the United States of America
Designed by Rita Lascaro

Contents

THREE

One

THE BRINK

Wynona Stone is having trouble broaching.
She likes to float. A quick sip now and then,
the one indulgence she can't not allow,

appeases. She felt surer in her skin
some years ago; things change. Don't ask her how.
It's not impossible to lose, with coaching,

your aim or sense of what you're shooting for.
Wynona Stone is having trouble broaching.
She tries to float; a stiff swig now and then

appeases some, though now arises more
than then. Today her mean-streak's kicking in.
She hates her job. She blames the jobs she quit

and jobs she didn't get. She blames *before*
and *some day soon*. She blames how much depends
on relatives, and how her next-worst choice

became the only out. Now she's a drawer
of knives, jammed shut. She blames the headset voice,
a fuzzy *Nona, no* she must ignore

while listing names—old flames and ex-best friends—
and hoping life has disappointed them.
It's tenuous. She wants to see beyond

the spite that casts her life in metaphor.
Wants to, but can't. Her mind's a rotten pond.
And doubt? A storm that's never not approaching.

A SCENE NOT MADE

A week from thirty-four, your wits and ends
get tied like flies. Wynona's casting lines,
hoping to reel in something she can save.
She tries to catch her mother at this age,
already hitched and stitched and wanting more
than what her roles required. Wynona tries,
but draws, instead, a memory like a boot.

> The front porch. Summer. Mrs. Stone in slacks,
> church shoes, some crabshack shirt. She's breaking in
> the shoes. And pacing. Thin-skinned, overbrowned,
> with sunken features like an apple doll.
> She waits for Mr. Stone. Or anyone.
> Her brow says, "Well." Her feet, though, hammer home
> the surer counterpoint. No sign of him.

> Wynona stays inside but looking out
> the window; in another century
> the room would be a drawing room. The Stones
> don't have a name for it, all shades of green,
> the carpets, drapes and moldings. Hideous.
> Wynona drives a stagecoach up and down
> the walls. Her right arm swings and skirts the sill,
> defying gravity. Patience, for her,
> is just a vehicle born on by whim.
> This is before she knows the difference
> between a noun and verb, but knows enough
> to figure something isn't happening.

> There's music in her mother's brooding pace,
> and in Wynona too, the motor's hum,
> dissembling their silence like a slip
> that zips to hide a cushion's ugly pattern.
> Still, girl-world's safer; she can turn around:

to drive is hope, and hope, a push like driving.
From floor to wall and back, she drives to coax
the meaning from the motion, saying—yes,
*and almost singing—*surface, surface, surface.

Stay put. Lunchtime,
alone, she nosed
the cubbyholes'
old totes and clothes
(her sentence: lost
and found, in can't-
be-still pose).
Turn around.
Unsound in sense,
she'd been a noun
while recess
went to verbs,
whence donned
a syntax hat
and, passive, sat
she parsing words.
Fell through the cracks
said they. Disbarred,
she tried *relax,*
then tried *too hard.*

AXIS

Decked out, half cat,
          half goddess (pen-
thin whiskers, cape,
          and jumprope tail)
Wynona bows
          to bless her luck:
a door that locks,
          a costume box,
a family not
          about to knock.

Belief begins
          with ritual
rehearsed: the way
          she waves a prism
occasioning
          the exorcism
of sawdust fauna,
          topless dolls,
the hero from
          an army set;

how, long before
          a note can stir
the mum balloon
          her brain contains,
she's finished growing
          singular,
exacting love
          for this world
she made herself
          the center of.

THE STONES

Wynona has two brothers. One's estranged.
The other lives in town. It's not her fault
she likes him less, though nobody's concerned
with her concerns. Estrangement, as it goes,
is not the sort of thing the Stones discuss.
At dinner Sundays, they talk moles. *We might
have moles,* they say. They talk potential moles
and porkchops. Charred? A greasy bark? Too charred?
A Stone might see a mole. They eat this way.

If Mrs. Stone turns cold—she often does:
the silent treatment, ruffled feathers, blahs—
they speak for or about her: *Mother likes
a darker char, don't you? You've cleaned your plate.
She has. She's happy.* As a last resort
Wynona or her brother maybe asks
their father, How's your this or that these days?
and he replies, *I've noticed an improvement*—
meaning, in something—shut up—anything.

PRESEASON

Knocked in the nose,
                    she buckled,
                                blinking black
with flashes
            like the impact. "Get your head
on straight,"
            her brother said
                        and turned his back
as she chased the ball
                    out of bounds,
                                still swallowing
the sting
        her braces pressed into her lips.

Weekends, the Stone kids practiced at the Y.

When league games ended
                        they could claim their half
a court;
        Wynona's brothers showed her off.

Under the lights' blue buzz,
                            they were her sure
opponents,
        big feet planted
                        at the key,
hands swatting
            when she dribbled,
                                stutter steps
and spin moves,
            trying to get by.
                            Along
the silver row
            of water fountains, men

who maybe, once,
        were stars unlaced
                their hi-tops,
t-shirts sagging
        with dark V's of sweat.
"Kid sister?"
        "Yep." They nodded,
                almost beaming,
while Wynona kept on,
        dizzy with a need
to please,
        each pass and rebound
                sinking in
as scent:
        leather and salt and hardwood wax.

But she preferred those mornings,
                buzzerless,
before the long shots
        counted, every move
chalked out,
        an X or O,
                defensive pressure
and broken lines—love
                she learned to receive
like a chest pass
        lobbed
                from the periphery.

OBJECT LESSON

The stock mythologies and fibs aside,
you wouldn't say the grown-up Stones had lied,

just built a sort of kid-proof shed for storing
truths dispensed with, willfully ignoring

the fact that even though they had the kids
at heart, at heart, the kids were normal kids

who worried most when anything appeared
too normal. Thus, their grandpa, as they feared,

was neither "sleeping late" nor "A-OK"
but dying in the upstairs hideaway.

They kept the secret, though, and said goodnight
or pushed their drawings toward the slat of light,

the day he left much like the day before
except, back home, the Stone kids cracked his door

and frozen by their own adrenaline,
they hovered, slight disciples taking in

a room astir. Among the shells of things—
balled tissues, tubes, the table's cups and rings—

the Stone kids touched, before they spooked and fled,
a long depression on the featherbed

like a snow angel without wings.

HOMILY

Here is the church, here is the steeple.
Here are the pews with gum underneath.
Here is the priest reusing a sermon;
here is the priest's wife, picking her teeth.

"Can we agree faith is contagious?
"The answer," he says, "is simple: we must."
Here is the window, here is the breeze;
here is the sunlight covered with dust.

Here is a way a kid doesn't listen:
sketching balloons or horrible wrecks,
whispering, *Please, I'm dying to go*,
firing blanks at bald spots and necks.

Held or released, we're all killing time.
Even the choir can't stay awake.
Here is the church, here is the steeple;
here is the exit congregants take.

Here is the priest reusing a sermon
(though this is hard to substantiate).
Can we agree faith is contagious,
passing a yawn or collection plate?

Here is the window, here is the breeze.
Surely it's over, most of us hope.
Here is a way a kid doesn't listen:
finger as barrel, knuckle as scope,

whispering, *Please, I'm dying to go*.
Here is impatience: dozens of hands,
held or released. We're all killing time.
Here is a way a kid understands.

PORTRAIT OF THE ARTIST WITH A C+

She suffered through the unease of Beginning
    Ceramics, Section Eight,
    and couldn't concentrate
in a dusty room where all the wheels were spinning

but hers. The teacher showed slide after slide
    depicting urns and challises
    from crumbled tombs and palaces.
A limewood likeness staring, waxy eyed,

was cut, he said, to fit the mummy's face
    and proved the ancients knew
    the body holds things too,
a sculpted vessel filled with empty space.

Wynona hardly heard him. Unconcerned
    with mimicking techniques
    of dead Pharaohs or Greeks,
she penciled grand designs while others learned

the classic forms of amphora and jars,
    but when it came to clay
    her hands got in the way,
and glazed, the goblet wobbled, nicked with scars.

So when, inside the kiln, it tipped and broke,
    she worked with what she had
    and for Christmas gave her dad
a lovely ashtray, though he didn't smoke.

BIOLOGY LESSON

The drummer from her brother's metal band
is planted in the floodlit driveway, jacked
off Mountain Dew or trucker speed or god

knows what. It's turning summer. You can hear—
even before you smell—things come alive,
the awful song: two parts pondwater, one

part rub and hum, and maybe this is why
he hunches down and tries to catch a frog.
Wynona watches from the hot garage

the way the drummer rises, rapt, before
it pisses in his grip. And when he flinches,
proves he's squeamish too, she thinks he sees

she saw. But here's her brother, dragging all
the inside light behind him, keys in hand,
halfway to gone. She's trying not to guess.

Tonight she'll make a Jell-O cell. He won't
come home, or he'll be late. Hypothesis:
it's no one's business where he went, or is.

SET PLAYS

The problem with the Lady Raiders? Raw
potential notwithstanding, their best skill
was getting rid of coaches, five so far:
the first a man who made them pick and roll
like guys, preferring guys; then someone's aunt
who had a boob tattoo—and, time would tell,
a felony; for several weeks a priest;
and then a college star who'd never been
alone with fifteen girls in sports bras, thick
as thieves, and mean, together far too miffed
to name the plays they wouldn't execute;

and then the civics teacher, scrawny, bald,
who bent the rules and maybe hadn't learned
the rules, who hung around a breath or two
too long and didn't seem surprised the night
the girls rebuffed his "huddle up," affecting,
collectively, the disaffected slump
of *I'm so freaking over this*, their last
defense a surly inner monologue—

even Wynona, once so full of drive,
a dynamo before the season tipped
towards loss. By then her split-screen mind refused
to listen to another bad excuse
for a pep talk, moving out of bounds, backstage,
where her best friend, she knew, was taking off
her shirt, coy Nina with a boy Trigorin,
an actress cast to play an actress acting—

"If you ever need my life, come and take it,"
a line Wynona helped her memorize.
And what she would've given for her own,
one sentence that could shut him up, this coach

who made his exit, sensing mutiny
was imminent, but didn't really leave:
he waited for her in the training room
with two fat bags of ice and, hushed beneath
the hum of dingy lights and washers wringing,
told her *honey, it'll all be fine,*
as if that wasn't what she told herself.

THE ROBOT HEAD

Wynona's brother left around the time
her fifth coach quit. A few good dads stepped in.
Preseason led to scrimmages, the fall
where all is crisp, still hanging on; then orange
exploded everywhere. That Halloween,
Wynona built a robot head. Her best
accessory, she wore it past the party,
first because she liked its heft—the strange
security, both conversation piece
and stopper—then because she'd grown attached
to feeling far from normal. At the house,
though Mrs. Stone forbade her, No you don't,
Wynona wore it anyway, her eyes
miotic through the holes, impervious,
just make me stop. Outside, the trees let go
in golden tones transformed to soupy grays;
Wynona wouldn't shed the robot head.
She propped it on the bleachers while she practiced
spin moves and strategies to beat the trap,
then put it on again. You'd be amazed
how long an act like this can last, if willed,
and it was finally Number Six who said,
Enough, Wynona, listen up. You think
it's funny? while Wynona blinked back, blank,
and didn't answer, *Funny? No one's laughing*.

By god, that's it;
don't try to set her straight.
She never said
she'd been upright
her whole life. Take
those kneepads, burned
like oven mitts,
those cheeks she's turned
and turned and turned—
no wonder, curbside
waiting on a ride,
Wynona's not
too broken up.
In seven seasons, all
she's learned is loss
involves perspective.
How big of her,
you might be thinking;
other times she might
agree: she's big
in certain circles.
Thrown to splotchy
farm girls, though,
she hedges, guaranteed
to catch an elbow
where it hurts,
and it hurts everywhere,
so nights like these,
the stars gone dim,
the sky a scoreboard
eyes can't read,
Wynona sighs,
By god, I quit,

a call God doesn't need:
Almighty Whistle Blower,
earth is just
his rattled seed.

ONE ON ONE

She meets him in the locker room, hot-dark
    and cranking after practice, teams
gone home, because there is a door, a couch.
    He doesn't mind her flush, his tongue
alive with salt, and what she feels is lost
    upon her thicker thoughts. *Like this*,
the headset voice keeps saying, *More like this*.
    A puffed up kid in giant pants,
he's slight. She's slightly slighter. You okay?
    he asks. Just tell me if you're not
okay. But no, she's fine; she's running over
    tape: her free-throw ritual,
the *dribble, dribble, dribble, cock, release*
    and follow-through, eyes on the air
above the hoop. There's really no excuse,
    said Number Six when she went one
for nine. Her head is always in the game
    until the game. A mental upset.
Do this. Like this. Are you okay? His touch:
    not fingers—frogs. He feels like frogs.
She should've showered, really no excuse,
    and when he whispers, Winnie Stone,
you're something, that's when she says stop, enough,
    and tired of reacting, takes
him, helpless, in her mouth. And lets the clock
    run down. And gets this over with.

A CHRISTMAS STORY

Wynona pleases well. *You shouldn't have*
she says, unwrapping. *Thank you* . . . overlapping
with Mr. Stone who drones, *You shouldn't have*
but thank you, did you see? to Mrs. Stone
who didn't see but says she did, then does.

Even the brothers, back when they were two
right shoes, had aced the gracious face but paled
next to Wynona. Queen of subtlety,
she punctuates the lulls. Here, holidays
are days when pleasing means not disappointing.

Before *you shouldn't have* she mastered glee,
the giddy gig, to fare absurdities
from enterprising elves to fairy hoarders—
myths she'd washed her hands of years before
she found the loot, heard muffled cussing, late,

as Mr. Stone bungled some unforeseen
assembly. Still, Wynona played along,
surprise reprised, half-understanding life
over and over would require this
belief in things after they don't exist.

SMOKE AND MIRRORS

Back then, girls teased their hair, big bangs
like loofahs on their foreheads. Plumes.
Somebody spiked the punch, they said,
as if they'd wanted plain old punch.

They shared their earrings, weed, and jeans,
wore underwear with satin bows,
and danced on stage while nights wore on
in shots and smoke—and on and on.

Back then, before the silly me
of retrospect, they reeked of yes,
diffusing through the bar to go
their separate ways the moment stay

awake or stick together seemed
impossible—demanding later
in the tone of frowning, *Tell
me everything.* They saw their share

of bunk beds, ancient futons, floors,
and dudes whose moves were easily
excused till dusty sunlight cut
the room in two. Then, sitting up

like damsels in a cuckoo clock,
they smoothed their tops and balled their socks,
said, *This we didn't do*, assured
what's missing isn't—can't be—true.

HIGHER EDUCATION

When college left her reckoning
chickens and eggs, Wynona's basket grew
unwieldy. Knowing what she knew
was wrong, she called her thesis "Cut the Mustard:
The Art of Scraping By," but failed
       to keep from getting flustered.

So, wrapped in half-learned ropes, she bailed
(major: Vocational Equivocation)
to take an overdue vacation.
She'd planned to shape up, travel, go to plays;
instead she ate coldcuts in bed
       watching the soaps most days.

She turned to meditation. Head
on fire, incense only clogged her nose,
oms more like *ums*; in lotus pose,
she wilted, chakras shot and compass sprung,
abandoning her mystic side
       and all the rumpus sung

on high. No longer unified,
she tried to cause a racket—silently—
with bumper sticker punditry
but, tactless in political affairs,
got honked at, mad, and had to face
       the rearview's angry glares.

At last, afraid to lose the race,
Wynona moved back home. She'd need a year,
she said, to find her rhythm here,
though waiting for the perfect key to strike her,
she found the songs she'd yet to sing
       would always sound more like her.

Two

DOWN AND OUT

Wynona Stone is having trouble broaching.
She'd hoped to float. A stiff swig usually
appeases. Not today, though, nosireee.

Lunchtime, she turns the soaps on, doesn't watch.
She eats ham slices, peeling from the pack,
and folds her clothes: a wad of poly-blends,

worn uniforms, a slip she can't take back
and so keeps washing, wishing it would shrink.
She is, by most accounts, a wishy-washer,

sanguine humor fading into pink
unmentionables. She thinks she needs a shot
of gusto, potent proof, or—*Nona, no*—

she needs another preposition: at
something, her shot should be. That's better, yes,
but what? A standard-issue happiness?

The headset voice: *Is that not what you had?*
Good question, thinks Wynona, maybe so:
she's not unhappy, but she's not unsad.

WELCOME TO PLEASANT BLUFF

It's not unpleasant here. The chicken plants
and car plants grow like plants. Here, all the sames
are different, though a hell-bent countenance
persists in yards supporting past elections
and latticed propane tanks. Here, names (like Jerry
of Jerry's Rigs) mean business; football games

mean war. Here, kids attend Dead President
Primary, right off Bigwig Avenue,
and strip malls flank the Holy Testament
(whose latest message, *God's grace gives us rage!*,
has lost the *c-o-u*); the new Corrections
Department borders Three Sons Barbeque

(run by two moms). Here, downtown is disguised:
the old P.O. a bank. The gallery
that used to be a mill, now capitalized
The Mill, sells space and photographs of mills.
Here, progress means, ostensibly, a stage
of reclamation, from topography

to toponymy. But since the genius lies
in places, not in names, here, once you're there,
you'll lack an actual to actualize,
finding no oaks in Oakmont Cemetery
and only shops in Walnut Square, no hills
in Eden Hills, no Eden—anywhere.

THE STONE HOUSE

Not speaking, having taken the position
of not my turn, they tune each other out
by tuning in tonight in separate rooms
with separate TV sets. For Mr. Stone,
another naval battle marathon.
For Mrs. Stone, a freak show reconceived
as *Miracles of Modern Medicine*.
It's volume versus volume. Volume wins.

The intercom their house is wired for
was always spotty; once the kids moved out
they let it die for good. Those years of fuzz
had simplified the rules of intercourse:
either you scream until somebody answers
or keep it to yourself and wait. And wait.

SLOW FADE

Wynona in a dress that doesn't fit:
the drape's all wrong, she looks like she's been hit

by a baby shower; plus her hair's a wreck—
think Shirley Temple on a rooftop deck

come late July. Wind smacks the tablecloths
and snuffs the votives; overzealous moths

self-immolate. *Well isn't this a bitch,*
she mutters, stiff-lipped. Though she's sure to ditch

the cordial shtick, a friend she's sampling
has taken her under an ample wing

which, fanning out this evening, spans a flock
of locals-about-town. Fine-feathered stock

(seersuckered, atomized), they're lovely, ripe
for conversation—not Wynona's type.

The plot unfolds, backwater roman-fleuve:
hand-shaking husbands, wives who say *make love*

as in "When Doug and I were making love,"
or "Doug made love to me," or "Doug, that love

we made was *really something*." Out of touch
with social cues, Wynona drinks too much—

which suits her role: the shoe about to drop.
Were she to belt "The Good Ship Lollipop"

they'd chuckle, *What a ham*, and, feeling smug,
rehash it after making love to Doug . . .

Instead, she whirls her glass, eviscerates
a napkin, little loves-me-nots, and waits

to find a way around the mise-en-scène.
No matter where she is, she's looking in

on someone else's story. That's the threat:
becoming extra on a crowded set.

Wynona wonders, *If you fill a space,
are you still extra?* but she holds her face

at whooptedoo; grinning chagrin intact,
a round of whooptedoo helps things contract,

and that's her super power: she'll demure
by shrinking what's about to swallow her.

THIS IS THE TOWN WYNONA BUILT

To call the thing a replica would be misleading. There are omissions, twists. The scale is off. Picture Wynona in a mirror holding up a nature shot. That's more like it. How it started, anyway. She said yes to the cow patties, no to the cows, yes to the silos and fences. She said no to the high school and museum and gym, yes to the two best beauty shops; no to the succulents, most types of moss, but yes and yes again to rocks—an impressive array of sizes and formations, crags and pebbles, slabs and cliffs. She scrapped the train but kept the tracks, snuffed stars to fit the orrery—how else to account for the sky, empty space? She picked the crops, no need for fields, and set each table with a meal but left the dining rooms implied. She drew the line at supers, cousins-once-removed, love letters, pills, and knickknack shelves. This cleared a space for her small self, who has, Wynona must concede, her own small sense of style. There are no homes. Homes take awhile.

DUPLEX

At 6 months in
and half-unpacked,
the spare room fat
with boxes stacked
like bricks from some
demolished city, home

is where one day
Wynona vows
she'll hang the hat
or route the cows
she doesn't have
the width for here; as half

the time she's pressed
to pay for cable,
what's living large?
A sturdy table,
fewer ghosts—
at best, a dinner guest.

ISOBARS

Wynona almost never thinks of sex,
and not because she isn't having any.
She's fine. If sex was at her fingertips
just itching to be had, she wouldn't tell
herself *you ought to keep your eye on that
at least*. Don't get her wrong, she's been swept up
in lust; she's fared some hot and heavy romps,
but none that ever added up to much
more than an *ah* or *uh* and then a lot
of *say what?* Thanks for asking, though. She's fine.
Her mind is occupied. She does Sudoku.
Meditates. She has the internet
and TV Guide and doesn't think of sex.
Not last week, not this morning, certainly
not right this second when the camera cuts
to the Weatherman, his Chiclet teeth agleam,
who says you better throw a blanket on
those roses, we're expecting record lows;
not even when he reaches out to read
the map his hand invents, though she'll admit
he makes her wish she was a continent.

UMPTEENTH SUPPER

Plattering last night's biscuits, lard like wax
across the top, with sausage pucks, a heap
of eggs, and coffee cooked

to diesel, Mrs. Stone has grown content
with gestures, thought that ought to count, and might
if she were thinking harder.

Here it sits, though, Sunday's larder, cold
before it hits the plate, and hardly colder
when the family's late.

So by the time they eat, it's no one's fault,
a table full of martyrs who, by god,
will finish what they're given,

leave no bones worth picking. Yes, it's tough
to be a Stone, so busy keeping score
they share the meal alone.

AUBADE

Dawn opens with a fog of cyclamen.
Wynona lets a little less light in,
drawing the drapes. *Oh, Monday.* Buses huff
and grumble, junking up the morning sounds,
so starting off she's rushed. With so much much,
Wynona wishes she could just adjust
the magnitude. But here it is: the world,
flexing its chest, all business, saying *Now!*
a move two lovers on the other shore
of urgency might manage to ignore.

THE MUSEUM OF THE WAY WE WERE

Defying class, the housewares cabinet
holds shark teeth, pearls, a hand-carved marionette,
two breast pumps, and nine rosewood plates—
         the only set extant
      in Pleasant Bluff. A placard states
         Pretty significant.

Beside it, shelves of velvet lined with tassels
are colonized by tiny pewter castles:
      every snuffbox ever owned
            by Mrs. M.E. Dorsett,
      whose great-grandchildren also loaned
         her next-best whalebone corset

but took it back. With business in decline
even the tri-state's largest ball of twine—
      part of a new addition billed
            the Trade and Labor Wing—
      could hardly draw the weaver's guild
         or kids from neighboring

school districts. This is why, today, we find
Wynona on a ladder, disinclined:
      she's dusting off the memory
            of battles lost, reclaimed
      in disengaged artillery
         and shells dug up, then framed.

INTERNAL REVIEW

Wynona's not what's called a perfect hire.
She tends to show a little too much id—
close-talking, looking people in the fly,
humming too hard. Her mode of skating by?
About as subtle as a giant squid.
At least she's fine with period attire.
At least she hasn't slapped a gifted kid,
or flashed her crack, or set the place on fire.

Regarding efforts toward diplomacy
she's vowed to ditch her jumbo headphones, shower
religiously, and follow all directions
from Lois, acting Head of Small Collections—
though (full disclosure) Lois wears her power
like a bad perfume. The air's so . . . *Loisy*
Wynona struggles, making less an hour
than what it costs to muster *woe is me.*

And who can blame her when she's made to play
the dulcimer, only a camera phone
from going viral (twice); or even worse,
when Lois lends her alto, every verse
a claim to greatness. There's no mood or tone
Wynona's spongy face won't give away.
She's better off off-season, left alone
to rage against the Wall of Macramé

or, just now, pour ammonia into bleach.
On a cleaning spree of sorts, still reeling from
the morning shift, Wynona's gripes eclipse
her oversight, and mop in hand, she slips

on her own slow shadow, thinking, *I've become
so strange* . . . Indeed, a self her feet can't breach:
top-heavy, arms like tentacles gone numb
from sensing what's forever out of reach.

DEPOSED

"Look, I'm not saying that I didn't sculpt a tiny model of the Weatherman in polymer clay. I absolutely did, and it was marvelous, no easy feat. You find me someone who can stripe a button-down and trefoil tie, forge cufflinks at matchbook scale, and I'll hairlip the Pope. It's true, too, I built a model of the station, but just the set, no cameras or talking heads; he needed context, don't we all. And— right again—I stuck the tiny Weatherman on the real Weatherman's car, upright like a hood ornament, no strings attached; and sure, I had to stake out the station, which took a week and several lenses, some of them illegal. But look, it was a gift I didn't rush; I shaved the jaw and neck bone, added props—poncho, barometer, wind tunnel—before arriving at munificence. Munificent and then some, and excuse me for living, it never crossed my mind he wouldn't be flattered, you tell me what's more flattering? So to suggest I've hopped the fence between propriety and private property, well that's the lowest blow. Maybe he wasn't keen to see things as they are, because, you know, I didn't glam it up; I left loose skin, the dented nose, the belly fat. I've had my fill of Davids, such muscle and junk, and I'll take the moles, the goiter, any day. And hey, I hear you, no one wants to be a creep, but you should ask him— let him cool off first, then ask the Weatherman when he was last immortalized. I bet you *never*'s what he'll say. So, look, I like to mess around with clay, but not for any other reason than I want to get the details right. It makes me feel, I don't know, like the gods must've felt—shaping nothing into something you can hold but never grasp."

HUMAN RESOURCES

Wynona ruins people, mixing parts
        of bodies parted with with parts
in progress. Like Madame Tussaud, she's not
        afraid to shave and re-allot
a heavy beard or simply fuse two guys
        (has-been and big shot on the rise),
to clip and transplant, strip a lady, gray,
        of her once glowing décolleté.
Even the model Weatherman was matched
        with pinkish forearms she detached
from what was Lover #12, a spare
        femur, and a former roommate's hair
(she may not save them but she always saves
        their shades). Afflatus comes in waves,
they say. Though very little change occurs
        among her minor characters
(more ornamental), few of those she's dated
        stick around—articulated.

FIRST STANDOFF

Old Flames vs. The Weatherman

They've formed a gang: the two-time champion
her girlfriends said was *awesome, really fun*;
the man of few words but an alphabet
of tics, who took her to Hawaii once,
despite her repertoire of cool affronts;
the boss who wanted kids and wouldn't let
her pay the check; the mental parasite
she's spent a decade trying to forget—
they know the ropes, and, folks, they're here to fight!
What are the odds this time they'll get it right?

But holding strong and sporting perfect diction
and teeth, and hair, Wynona's favorite fiction:
the Weatherman! Who's unafraid to tell
three counties where the wind's about to blow
and be wrong! Who knows twenty words for snow
and, safe to say, has never not slept well,
appeased by rain or good publicity;
whose smooth equivocations will dispel
any improbable with *probably*;
who's swirling in the eye of *wait and see*.

WYNONA'S COSMETOLOGIST

Pink perm rod puckered like a cigarette,
she lisps a little as she combs and rolls,
and doesn't care who waits. She's overbooked:
one in the chair; a row of patient souls

with heads in driers; several draped in smocks
like mutant jellyfish. The rest, sardines,
fill up the wicker loveseats, glad to chat
or eavesdrop, scanning last year's magazines.

She's talking to the mirror when she talks,
its surface framed with photos: kids as cute
as tutus, kickers, cloggers, dough-faced babies,
bow-head babies, babies dressed like fruit,

all wallet-sized. A sign above her lists
the fees for cut and color, manicures
and waxing ("brows and pits, *bikinis extra*").
She draws good tips, although the job secures

itself: the dos must be redone, new shades
of blond or bronze ("If you can't tone it, tan it!").
In here, the atmosphere, abuzz with heat
and aerosol, suggests a cozy planet

outside of time. Forget the yawning gods,
she plugs a clear cosmology: big bangs
are out, she says, try layers; fringe benefits
a puffy face, revives a mop that hangs,

exhausted. Mostly, though, she helps control
old damage. Sure, she'll hide dark roots or chop
dead ends, but she won't promise miracles:
nobody's reborn in a beauty shop.

LAUNDRY SONG

Woe to the grass-stained knees and sweater balls,
      popped flies and skoal rings, faded knits
and bleeding knits; woe to the extra smalls

stretched extra large, the labyrinthine runs
      in nylons, all the yellow pits
unbleachable: a closet's skeletons.

Since water won't dissolve a greasy spot,
      nor care repair a cross-stitched sham
whose X's void the optimistic plot

of *home sweet home*; since guests will make a mess
      of Christmas linens, slinging ham
and Jell-O salad, and it's hard to dress

for Jell-O salad; since whatever spills
      is full and—always—falling toast
lands on the buttered side, woe to the frills

and folds, the slips that can't be taken back,
      the suits with inkblots diagnosed
too late (best suited for the clearance rack);

woe to the silky underthings gone gray,
      the see-through duds that passed for posh
until their hidden seams began to fray—

and woe to launderers who blame design,
      too worn themselves to mend or wash
their dirty layers strung along the line.

INTERLUDE

She's playing hooky for the umpteenth lunch
this month, pure lust—blowing the Weatherman,
to put it bluntly. Days when he's off-screen
he calls and she comes running. Worth the risk,
she says, to hear him whistle, *Back that up
Wynona, let me feel you*—just some lip
the boom boys taught him. Isn't he a trip?
she says. They'd rendezvous, an alp or coast,
if time was not the essence, if between
these visits lines were clearer. They'd be seen

together if they weren't such public people,
but he's contractual. He mugs and points
at ghost maps, posits *partly probably*,
and waves his fingers, miming *smidge of drizzle*.
Meanwhile she clocks in; showing curios
to crones and chaperones, she makes a case
for *way back*, plus or minus *when*. They face
some hurdles, sure, she says, but once alone
they're who they are, agreeing constancy
would suit them if it came more easily.

On Channel 5, he's got a Grecian sheen,
a pocket square, a voice without a past;
in living color, those fronts disappear.
They hunker in his outskirts. There's a pond,
a kudzu sanctuary, ducks to feed.
So when the headset voice gets huffy—*Stay
another minute, you'll have hell to pay*—
Wynona doesn't budge. To snuff the ghosts
of repercussion, all she has to hear
is there's a chance tomorrow will be clear.

ALMIGHTY VAST ETCETERA,

My faith in you has been renewed.
I'm throwing up with gratitude.
I've made my peace with espadrilles.
I've traded savings bonds for bills
and lemongrass for Diet Rite.
Resolved to give the run around
less often, I vow not to loan
my car to strangers, mow the lawn
in lingerie, or try to sound
important. Envy's good as gone
for good, and when in doubt I've found
examining my cellulite
at night while singing *My Sharona*
really puts a damper on
the schadenfreude. See? I've grown.

Lost cause my ass,
Wynona Stone

SECOND STANDOFF

Wynona vs. Lois

Lights up: The Museum of the Way We Were.
WYNONA, corseted, a character
about to break: she's . . . well, just standing there.
Her bonnet flops and makes her face a dim
capitulum, her slumping frame the stem.
An expert sulker, prone to whisper-swear,
most weekends she leads long historic tours
for the sort of people history ignores.
Nobody has to tell her life's not fair.

A clomping beat precedes the shadow thrown
by LOIS, closing in: "Wynona Stone."
Built like a chicken (or an egg—on stilts),
she reaches up to finger-dust a sconce.
Being woman fond of provenance
and neat display, a woman who finds quilts
exciting, when she eyes the butter molds
askew, her jaw goes tight. Her silence holds
a charge. And right on cue, Wynona wilts.

HOSPITALITY

The days of dainty napery,
   salt bowls, and centerpieces
are done. Foreclosed, a home's a house;
   here, signs say *short-term leases*.

The royal treatment? Who has time?
   Box wine, a deli platter,
and it's a party—not to say
   decorum doesn't matter

in Pleasant Bluff, just people's sense
   of reciprocity
has changed—from canine palaces
   adorned with filigree

and eaves, to little knitted caps
   fitted to pickle jars,
sympathy hams, or Christmas wreaths
   in the grills of burnt-out cars.

That's why, despite her wild hairs,
   Wynona aims to bring
a sense of old Colonial style
   to the latest next big thing:

when others at the beauty shop
   choose lighting bolts or hearts,
she asks the cosmetologist
   to wax her lady parts

and leave a pineapple design
   (which, once the splotches fade,
looks something like a monkey paw,
   maybe a hand grenade).

But either way, the Weatherman
                doesn't say a word,
just flaps against Wynona's lintel
                like a manic bird,

until she understands he'll never
                give a hoot about
the logic of her welcome, though
                he gladly wears it out.

COME TO THINK OF IT

The way he got excited
lying in her bed
explaining jazz
was not the compliment
she took it as.

WYNONA TAKES FIVE

But let's be honest: she was gone for more
like fifty. Nothing she's not done before;
so what? She'd been to see the Weatherman
discuss the rise of melanoma. ("Tan
means vulnerable," he said—which she'll admit
was not that hot. You take what you can get.)
Wynona thinks, as far as time's concerned,
you have to steal or kill. This hasn't earned
too many points with Lois, whose two cents,
unsparing, tends to be at her expense.

Lois gives off, in no uncertain terms,
the air of someone prone to combat—germs,
ant colonies, the bulge, untethered babies,
a life of probably nots disguised as maybes . . .
So it's a shame Wynona, running late
this afternoon, will overestimate
her ability to shapeshift, finding that
she can't. Transparent in her tricorn hat,
she sidles up the back porch, unaware
of Lois watching from a giant chair
that looks like wicker's answer to a throne.
She gives a righteous *humph*: "Wynona Stone."
Wynona: "Butt out."
                                        Lois *humphs* again
and swings her head, equine. "Did I butt in?"

Another day, she might've wished her harm
or made her likeness out of clay—one arm
a full hand longer, thick hips, overbite—
then sliced her into pieces. She still might,
but not today. No, almost dignified,
Wynona airs her laundry on the side
of caution, telling Lois, *Lois, this*

just isn't working out. For emphasis
she adds, *you bitch.* She's stayed too long is why
she'd rather board the train it takes to try
than wait for *soon.* It's time she called time's bluff,
and soon, she says, is never now enough.

THE HIATUS

She spent it mad. She spent it trying hard
to get a handle. She had several
approaches. Handle-getting was an art.
She built another model of herself
then drove her out of town. She read two acts
of a 5-act play. She tooled around in large
and unbecoming hats, studied her face
and practiced looking stoic. Grateful. Wise.
She wiled away whole mornings, blurred, unsure
what sort of handle she was reaching for.
She'd been a kid with brilliant stickers, saved,
unstuck, in want of one deserving surface
that never surfaced, a girl with stomachaches
developing, despite the no-you're-fines,
the it's-just-in-your-heads, a real hard knot
of worry, normal as another organ.
She'd been a shrunken woman dressed to kill
on a rooftop deck, then puking overboard
right after lifting up her blue blue dress
to please a not-man, boy as boy can be.
She'd been a noun rehearsing prepositions:
against a cliff, above a line; in planes,
on buses—always pining for the stop
where some new plot or you was waiting, poised
to wave her in from the percussive hum
of her own head. But these past-perfect I's
had been, she came to understand, a ruse,
a way to grip the present where she spent
her long hiatus looking back, and saw
she was all of them, still. Is all of them.

Three

HIBERNACULUM

A cold snap: so Wynona isn't broaching.
Her sighs form sullen bubbles on the ceiling,
impervious to sun. It wears her out,

this rut she's in. At least when she was reeling
she had a line. Lately, she's come to doubt
her tactics, all that effort slinging mud

to wallow in it. Could she actualize
a cool detachment—like the hard-shelled buds
of certain pond plants, which, designed to sink

and spend the winter in the benthos, rise
in bloom each spring—Wynona wouldn't mind
the darker months. Instead, etiolated,

approaching dormancy, she can't unwind.
While she'll admit she needs a simile
like she needs a lead balloon, heavily-weighted,

sometimes a simile is her best shot
to see things as they are. The rotten weather
is not Wynona's problem: like a knot,

her heart's pulled taut inside this self she's spun,
and, like a knot, what's holding her together
is the energy she'd need to come undone.

THE SOAPS

Recessed, the kitchen fixture blinks, one wing
or thorax shy of shorting. *Well, good morning,*
says Wynona as the lit eye huffs
to get the percolator up to here-
we-go-again. Then, there it goes again.

Across the island she can barely see
the television screen but leaves it on
through news and talk shows, anxious for the soaps.
Amnesia, wrecks, emotive sex—she's washed
her hands of are you kidding, having found

it's mostly variations on a theme,
as when a woman loves a man who's not
the man she thinks he is—or learns, too late,
the man who is the man she thought the one
who isn't was, believes he's someone else.

THE DIABETES LUAU

Arriving late amid a haze
    of leis and beachwear clinging
to cheeks and cleavage, floral prints
    so loud her eyes are ringing,

Wynona motors through the crowd
    and hums the theme from JAWS.
She doesn't stop to thank the hosts;
    a far more worthy cause

has pulled her here, already burnt
    as, daiquiri in hand,
she gets back in the daiquiri line.
    There's nothing she can't stand

like pool-side people trying hard
    to suck it in and flex,
but, resolute, she walks the length
    from deep to shallow, checks

the bodies flopped on flaccid floats
    or stacked for chicken fights;
she sidesteps ukuleles, blowup
    sharks, and socialites,

and while her muumuu fans the flow
    of traffic like a sail,
Wynona fares the cramped veranda—
    there, leaned on a rail,

at once she finds the Weatherman
    and knows she's lost him too:
wearing a partly sunny smile,
    he plucks his cocktail's blue

umbrella, spears her ponytail,
    and mumbles, turning red,
Voilà! as if this might forestall
    the thunder in her head.

WYNONA WORRIES

She'll never use the word adagio.
A wreck of self, of nervy tics and torque,
she'll spend her tenure at the fireworks show
not thinking *cherry blossom, jellyfish*
but *grass gives me a butt rash* and *I wish
I hadn't had that second plate of pork.*

She's grown untenable. Her slump concedes
the sure discomfiture of Wonder Bras
and wooden pews. She can't say what she needs
but knows the wash-that-man-right-out shampoo
has done a number on her luster too,
and what she'd called a classic case of blahs

is in her blood. Her gut's a boiler room.
She wakes in haze and flirts with vertigo,
excusing truths: that she's been groomed for gloom;
that, lecherous for what she can't possess,
she's left with fantasies—like faith, a yes
she conjures while her doubt is groping no.

PALINODE

You might've heard
she built a throng,
clay figures, squat
as shotgun shells,
her long lost foes
and loves gone wrong,
then stood them up
like dominoes,
pushed one and watched
the others fall,
said, *Are you pretties
pitiful or what?*
Call it a rut.

You might've heard
she made a scene,
ordained a deacon
in the Church
of Mean, but really,
that's not right,
for rung for rung
hers was a softer spite.

She never clipped
their spine's short wicks
nor mashed a knee
deliberately;
in fact she gave
her Adams Eves,
said, *Hey, we all
need company—*
no spite in that

to speak of, though
it's true she tucked
a headless fetus in
a womb or two.

WYNONA MAKES LIKE A TREE

That is, stays put,
one root per foot,
until, thick-skinned, she sings,
Only a sucker
lets love pluck her.
Sass, she hopes,
will mask the taste
of grim complicity
in case her air
unleaving there
conveys an ancient haste:
less tree, more bush
that used to be
a woman someone chased.

SECOND OPINIONS

"Right, right, Miss Stone, that's good, I see,"
explains the guru/analyst
Wynona visits to untwist
her nerves and rectify her chi.

"Like this?" She scans his office, lined
with cheap batik and natal charts.
"Right, right," he says (writes: *fidgets, darts;*
writes: *not like that*). "Just try to find

a blank space, nothing in the way,
okay?" Wynona nods but starts,
as usual, to make a mess
of orders. Though she hears him say,

"Count backwards; think of breaths, not clocks,"
she's wet with sweat and must confess
her spine aches and her body's less
a temple than a tinderbox—

to which the guru shakes his head.
He mutes the boombox, caps his pen,
says, "Fine. We'll shoot for next week, then."
Prognosis? *Hanging by a thread.*

SELF-CHECKOUT

The paradox of choice: supply demands
variety, but just how many brands
of waffles does a woman need to test
Before selecting one that suits her best?
From waffles on to syrup (which entails
the nuances of sausage links, and sales),
it's awful. Though Wynona hopes to build
her option-tolerance, last week she killed
a morning, slack-jawed, at the hardware store
trying to pick the perfect two-by-four-
inch strip of cardstock (teal a tad too jade,
luna too mucus, golf course lacking glade,
only to find her subtle English pea,
wall-sized, was not so subtle). You can see
why after several minutes making faces
at her reflection in the freezer cases
this afternoon, she simply calls it quits—
to hell with waffles, butter, bacon bits—
and drops her basket in the sea of feet
like a bomb or baby. Sure, she needs to eat,
would maybe call for takeout could she spin
the order without going in again.
As for delivery, it sounds terrific
prior to toppings ("Ma'am, please be specific,
which kind of crust?"), and drive-through joints divide
their menu into menus: pick a side,
pick three, in fact. No thank you, that's alright,
Wynona says. She's lost her appetite,
flat dithered out. So—barely getting by—
why won't she make a move to simplify?
She'd like to think that if she had her druthers
she'd ditch the druthers. Not so: like the others

who stand, eyes glazing over, and assay
the stock, Wynona hates to look away,
believes if she could memorize the list
she'd know there's nothing more than this she missed.

SONG FOR LAYING ODDS

She sings but not
for singing's sake.
She sings to say she's raised
the stakes, so all
or nothing means
no looking back, or breaks.
Risk is a mine
and she will dig.
The truth? You wrestle with
a pig, you'll wind up
sore or filthy;
bet against the devil,
your best shot
turns mighty dark.
She plays her cards alright,
but drawing one
last spark of fight,
she marries sure with wary,
sings, "Lucifer,
I see your light
and raise you a canary."

WYNONA'S DEAD FRIEND NANCY

When Nancy was alive, she wasn't good,
the sort who broke the rules because she could.
She had no boundaries and a nasty mouth,
and once her moral compass pointed south
it stuck there. Riding high on the dark horse
of waywardness, she never found a course
she couldn't stray from. As for golden rules,
she pawned them; as for love's unsuffered fools
she left a glut, sad-swooning. Necromancer
and harpy, succubus and table dancer,
she'd charm the pants off Jesus, people said.
First she went missing, then she turned up dead,
and no one sent a card or called the florist
except Wynona, left in life's dim forest
alone. She'd always trusted Nancy's lead,
a friend so surely doomed she saw no need
for rectitude—and didn't sugarcoat.
So when dread set its piston in her throat,
Wynona cracked a window, lit a candle,
said, "Nancy, sister, help me get a handle,"
and she appeared, like smoke inside a net:
"Wynona, hi," a voice familiar, yet
calmer.
            Wynona said, "A pantomime,
that's what my life's become. See, every time
I'm sitting pretty I'm compelled to spin
a web of spite, my most unsightly sin.
I've wished some awful wishes; I'd repent
if I could just decide which threads I meant.
It's difficult to broach; my thinking stalls,
and lately I'm the one inside the walls
of lonely. Tell me, am I—in your view—
on the guest list at Satan's barbeque?"
And Nancy answered, "Honey, that's a crude

perspective on the vast vicissitude
of death. I can't say how you'll pay for spite
or sass, and, listen, I'm no proselyte,
but I'll assure you this: if you think hell
means monkey demons or a roach motel,
then you're mistaken. Bodies come undone;
what won't dissolve, *that's* hell, the rusts of pride,
the sticky guilt. But there's a brighter side:
nobody fries. Since death, like art, is long—
just ask the prophets with their heads on wrong—
all bets are off. From sorry sons of guns
to straighter-shooting fathers, tramps to nuns
who never kicked the habit, dying single:
post mortem, as on earth, we intermingle.
It's quite the party."

                    "You mean everyone
ends up in paradise?"

                    "Technically, yes.
It's just that some of us enjoy it less."

BRAIN, STORM

Missing the Weatherman
this morning, she invents a storm, the sort
without a center where the wind's the worst,
that, rather, stretches as if trying to
get comfortable. Wynona's never been
much good at letting thoughts resolve themselves.
A storm, she thinks, needs landscape to dismantle,
and landscape needs a figure seeking cover.

Missing the Weatherman
this morning, she invents an isthmus, not
a sea in sight, and places at its edge
a lady unaware of what she's missing
or simply missing nothing while the clouds
well up like clouds, reminding her of clouds.

DEUS EX MACHINA

Not pillage, more
like disassembly, really,
since Wynona must
dissemble any figures
that resemble symbols:
calling this her last
sure sorrow, now she'll shut
the door on yesterdays
spent wishing for tomorrow.
No, she doesn't pillory
or pillage, merely drops
the model village, piece
by piece, into a coffee can,
says so long suckers
to the slips and scratches
of a universe produced
in batches, soon reduced
to a small heap she'll keep
concealed, a backup plan,
at least until she understands
art's less about this world
undone than how
she'll build another one.

CALCULATING ROUTE

Looking like Lady Liberty
      in a mud mask worn thin
that the cosmetologist prescribed
      for combination skin,

wearing a slip she calls a dress
      (it's clearly not), one sock,
one shoe, her hair heaped up, her free
      hand covering the clock,

Wynona drives a loop around
      a town two towns removed
from Pleasant Bluff—just up and left
      tonight as if that proved

she isn't stuck. Yes, see how stuck
      she isn't, unconcerned
with the vaguely British voice explaining
      where she should've turned?

She used to choose the scenic views,
      parked, flinging cans or matches
over the edge, relieved at last
      to see the purple patches

of sky go black; she used to feel
      half-holy, set apart
from the tangled arteries that fed
      the city's dim-lit heart.

Ah well, Wynona's older now
      and Holy's flown the coop;
she hauls her fat soul down the road,
      grown sick of chicken soup

and goodwill. These days, sleep's a hint
　　　her body doesn't drop,
and bloodshot, spray-tanned, flaky-faced,
　　　Wynona drives to stop

the endless spinning; nothing clears
　　　her head quite like the fogged
observatory of her car.
　　　Considering she's logged

a million miles on the stretch
　　　connecting Back and Forth,
she knows this much: from plate tectonics
　　　to magnetic north

the earth is shifty. Like the lost
　　　GPS in her lap,
the gods, those bum cartographers,
　　　are all over the map.

THIRD STANDOFF

The Headset Voice vs. Wynona

So you wanted rum with bossa nova, not
a snare drum, not your uncle's chilidogs;
wanted a big job, big deal, big ideas,
a title worth its tonnage on the tongue;
you wanted win-win worry, legs for days,
less box fan, much more circulation—fine.
Want all you want, it doesn't change a thing
about your perm, how even as we speak
your waves engage another decade, poofed
from haze and rain like platinum cotton candy;
it doesn't change a thing about the rain,
the pistol in your brother's glove compartment,
and how you never would've voted gauche
the theme of this, your thirty-somethingth birthday.
Your cousin JJ's staring at your chest.
You're wearing your old Lady Raiders shorts,
and all the first-team trophies time can hold
won't make you love the game the way you did
those first long summers when you played with ghosts
and won. Do-over is the single wish
most candles can attest to, but it's best
to lighten up. You really shouldn't screen
your calls by saying "I'm afraid she's dead."
Your not enough is someone else's much
too much, and celebrations aren't exempt
from dread. So have an icing rose and know
the swollen note too heavy for your throat
may well be hope, whose gaudiest disguise
is pride, and you can choke it down from here
to kingdom come, or you can muster up
the gracious face it takes to see the worst

has yet to be conceived—the running sum
of what's gone wrong and going wrong is just
a twinkle in the eye of everything.

DELETED SCENES

Wynona carrying the torch;
       Wynona on a float.
Wynona in a sandwich board
       with one side urging, "Vote

Wynona," and the other, "Don't."
       Wynona as the star
of *Wynona Stone, the Musical,*
       playing her avatar.

Wynona close to victory;
       Wynona in a crown;
Wynona, hidden, fiddling
       as Pleasant Bluff burns down.

Wynona on a unicycle;
       Wynona going pro;
Wynona someplace tropical,
       the Weatherman in tow,

or catapulted, zero G,
       to reach a future date
when, opening her time machine,
       she sets the record straight.

Wynona with a three-tier trophy,
       world's best boss or daughter;
Wynona in a life preserver
       rising from the water

on skis while, all aboard, the Stones
       take off across the lake,
Wynona sore but hanging on—
       and happy—in their wake.

ARTS AND CRAFTS

She did the MoMA
once but griped
those drooping clocks
weren't worth the hype.

Surreal? Big deal.
It's poppycock,
she said, best fit
for gift shop stock.

If time is fluid—
not seen, felt—
would memory make
a seen clock melt?

No, memory's too
ethereal—
Wynona needs
material

with edges, surer
shapes that hold
a crease or secret
triplefold,

and maybe (maybe)
this explains
the origami
cranes she hangs

whose patterned surface
somehow curbs
mimesis—crafts
less nouns than verbs.

Her masterwork
may never be
considered museum
quality,

among the high arts,
hard on strings,
that root for concepts
over things,

but bending wings
just so, she'd swear
with paper birds
she makes the air.

Acknowledgments

Acknowledgment is made to the following publications for poems that first appeared in them, sometimes in slightly different form.

32 Poems: "Laundry Song" and "Smoke and Mirrors"

Atlanta Review: "Preseason"

Blackbird: "A Christmas Story," "Deleted Scenes," Down and Out," "Hibernaculum," "Deposed," "Isobars," "A Scene Not Made," "Self-Checkout," and "Wynona's Hiatus"

Cavalier Literary Couture: "The Brink," "Grammar School," and "The Stones"

Evansville Review: "Arts and Crafts"

The Journal: "Slow Fade" and "This is the Town Wynona Built"

Kenyon Review: "Welcome to Pleasant Bluff"

Memorious: "Calculating Route," "The Cosmetologist," and "Hospitality"

Mississippi Review: "One on One," "The Robot Head," and "Set Plays"

Pembroke Magazine: "Second Standoff"

Poetry Daily (reprints): "Smoke and Mirrors" and "Welcome to Pleasant Bluff"

Phantom Limb: "Wynona Worries"

Sewanee Theological Review: "Aubade," "The Museum on the Square," "Portrait of the Artist with a C+," "The Stone House," and "Object Lesson"

storySouth: "Axis," "Brain, Storm," and "Duplex"

Subtropics: "Higher Education" and "Wynona's Dead Friend Nancy"

Tirage Monthly: "Almighty Vast Etcetera," "Second Opinions," and "The Soaps"

I'm very grateful to the Sewanee Writers' Conference, the University of Cincinnati, the Charles Phelps Taft Research Center, the Trustees of the Robert Frost Farm, and Rhodes College for generous financial support that helped me complete this book.

Thank you to Don Bogen, Jim Cummins, John Drury, Joanie Mackowski, Tim O'Keefe, Freeman Rogers, and Greg Williamson, who read early drafts and offered a heap of good advice; to Carrie Guss, my favorite cover artist; and to the crew at Persea Books, especially Gabe Fried.

Finally, three cheers and more for my family: Mom, Dad, Matt, Lisa, and the Wilkinson, Sisk, and Baird clans; and my friends, especially Leigh Anne Couch, Catherine Daly, Julia Delacroix, Jake Ricafrente, Sarah Trudgeon, and Kevin Wilson.